THRESHOLD

D0043854

Also by Shirley Kaufman

POETRY

The Floor Keeps Turning

Gold Country

*Looking at Henry Moore's Elephant Skull Etchings in
    Jerusalem During the War*

From One Life to Another

Claims

Rivers of Salt

Roots in the Air: New & Selected Poems

Mehayim Lehayim Aherim (selected poems in Hebrew),
    translated by Aharon Shabtai, Dan Pagis, and
    Dan Miron

Un Abri pour nos têtes (selected poems in French),
    translated by Claude Vigée

TRANSLATIONS

A Canopy in the Desert, poems by Abba Kovner

My Little Sister and Selected Poems, poems by Abba Kovner

The Light of Lost Suns, poems by Amir Gilboa

But What: Selected Poems of Judith Herzberg

The Flower of Anarchy: Selected Poems of Meir Wieseltier

ANTHOLOGY

*The Defiant Muse: Hebrew Feminist Poems from Antiquity
    to the Present* (co-edited with Galit Hasan-Rokem
    and Tamar S. Hess)

THRESHOLD

SHIRLEY KAUFMAN

Copper Canyon Press

Cover art: *Sun and Moon Space,* photograph by Robert Polidori, copyright by James Turrell. Installation view, Roden Crater, Arizona. The photograph was originally published in *The New Yorker.*

Copper Canyon Press is in residence under the auspices of the Centrum Foundation at Fort Worden State Park in Port Townsend, Washington. Centrum sponsors artist residencies, education workshops for Washington State students and teachers, Blues, Jazz, and Fiddle Tunes festivals, classical music performances, and the Port Townsend Writers' Conference.

LIBRARY OF CONGRESS CATALOGING-IN-PUBLICATION DATA

Kaufman, Shirley.
Threshold: poems / by Shirley Kaufman.
  p. cm.
ISBN 1-55659-192-6 (alk. paper)
1. Jerusalem — Poetry. 2. Palestinian Arabs — Poetry. 3. Jews — Poetry.
I. Title.
PS3561.A862T48 2003
811'.54 — DC21

2002154676

9 8 7 6 5 4 3 2

FIRST PRINTING

COPPER CANYON PRESS
Post Office Box 271
Port Townsend, Washington 98368
www.coppercanyonpress.org

for Bill
through it all

CONTENTS

One: Threshold

Three

Four

Five

ONE:

Threshold

...things will change:
you may even learn to live with what

has already happened: that will be
a new start...

A.R. AMMONS

You have to begin
with the word itself
                    first
tread of oxen

fury of
        threshing

stems
        and the husks of grain

to separate seed from straw
until

        the lifting of the new bride
over

                        white veil
                    floating and her
something blue

                    over the threshold
as in setting forth

                        without condition

the point where what you feel
is danger

threshold
　　　　of pain

or of wind's wildness

　　　　　　　desire
still felt or is it
(not less)

　　　remembered

IN JERUSALEM

split on the fault line

So many zeros
brimming with smoke

I had meant to say hope

explosions of
hope

    electric confetti
the night like a psychedelic fish tank
millions of jeweled sperm
                  swimming
over our cities
        millennium hype

threshold of
        what

        of having
and watching it go

the twenty-first century
            nothing
but sparks and flashes
          collapsed
into dust

      too many zeros
ending with smoke

New Year's Eve

The pines on our street
                            sway
from the waist
                light
on their shoulders
like a fringed shawl

the gardener
                kneels
toward the east at noon

touches his forehead
to the ground

                I watch
from my window

you are writing a book called
The Divided Heroine

                while I
am not in
                an English novel

                            trying
to put two parts of a life

together
                where they both
belong

        simmering

              rift

in the desert

          Sarah and Hagar

not

    Tess and Cathy

              two halves

of an ancient slippage

             split

on the fault line

Our neighbor in charge of the

shelter says

he'll clean it

sometime

before

the next war

we leave the door open
so he won't forget

each morning your sloping

shoulders

your resourceful hands your
fingers

ten flavors

of yogurt

labeled in Hebrew

if your knees were your hands
they would forget

their thick-rooted

pain

forget the headlines
reckless words

I shove

under the table

rub out

with my bare feet

All over Rehavia there are
tiny gardens
        green on the corners
in somebody's memory

            the name
incised on a concrete slab
           and a bench
with two immovable doves

blooms are staggered
           even in winter
when cyclamen jiggle the earth
and then the freesia

        stopping
to rest
    at the end of my block
two elderly women stare
straight ahead
      without speaking

hands folded
under their elbows

        coming undone
a little
    like braided straw
from too much handling

          too many

losses in Europe
        or here

wind bruises
          their delicate foreheads
their skin
        the color of water on sand
when summer is over
the shore undazzled

          and all the children
have gone back to school

You can feel the rising like a loaf
in the oven he says
                                    but it's not quite that

his fingers
                    lengthening my back
my neck
                holding the rest of me
                                                up
head
            floating

                            so that I walk through
sliding doors
                        and the world
slides past me

                    door and lintel
of the Japanese poems: the wooden frame
shaping the opening and the opening
shaping the frame

                            pine tree
blue plumbago over the wall
the red hibiscus

                            passing behind me
as I pass

the way a thought breaks off
in the *mind-heart* making

                                        space
          for another

                              no pond where I live
          there's no
                              frog splashing

          but
                              the old stones
                              lizard darts
                              sound of sunlight

          what goes   what stays

          the hearth-fire the aliveness
          at the center of the house

                    for Dan Armon and Jane Hirshfield

So we got out of Lebanon
out of the *botz*   the mud

bitter
         dregs at the bottom
when the cup
                   smashed

border
        as threshold

                       what now
pressing against the barbed wire
whose flags
                blue star burning
and stones
                (*it was fun* said
the professor)

what scrupulous anxiety
                                hovers
over the usual

            jay
its loud abrasive cry
in our jacaranda
                kiew kiew

why doesn't he sing why
does he sit there

                    whole
in his unbleached body

steak-knife tail dazzle of
                                blue
where the wing starts

repeating
            his screech his
portentous scold

                    iyew iyew

                            May 24

And you on my birthday

                           bonsai
little dwarf holding out
its arms
        tiny bulges of green

leaves swollen with love
for *you are remarkable*

                      even
spelling it out as she
                famously

let me
        count the
               ways

counting the candles
uncorking the wine

                  long-distance
runners
        pacing ourselves
for the finish

          but the bonsai
is crippled

        this is not
about binding

                              it's trying
              to tell me about
                              compression

              that less is

              like writing the Lord's
              Prayer
                    on a grain of rice

                                        June 5

New translation of Tsvetayeva

her photograph

             could be the same

as the young woman on my wall

slight

      tilt of the head

              her eyes

and my mother's

          dark soil

loamy

      and freshly turned

their apprehensive smiles

their loose curls

          falling

unpinned

     to their shoulders

locked herself

out of the house once

          stillborn

Russian poet

       my mother

trimmed the dead roses

sprayed poison on the ants

red ants red roses
                        and the fetus
flushed down the toilet

so even the absence
                        of red
stayed red in her mind

the door slammed shut before
she remembered

                she couldn't get in

Yahrzeit
June 21

Ripple of voices around the bed
I am listening
                to my own breath
listening
        to transcribed
voices

        the patient is stuck
not worse not better

                        a story
that will not unfold
                we do (did) *want*
her mood to improve

asthma   brain tumor   bone fractures
                        seizures   blood clots

around the bed

                        what's left
but *dignity*
        yes (no)

WITH DIGNITY
                        what they want
for themselves

but the comatose (not quite)
patient who opens her eyes

to
　　her name
　　　　　　　　　　what
does she
　　　　want

ventilator　　　stomach tube　　　morphine drip

who will pull out the

　　　　　　　　　design the

letting her go
　　　　　　　　they have decided

this is what Ann wants

　　　　　　　　　　　　to *go*
with dignity

　　　　　　　only one nurse
can say the unmentionable

he'll be up here at five to do the death

and it sounds like a song
or a dance

　　　　　　　I can almost
hear Elvis

c'mon and do do do

what we're doing

doin' the death

yeah

what are we doing

she opens her eyes

and stares

at the doctor

for Sharon

The trouble with anger

                          or with hate

is that it spills all over

                    won't

be contained

                  all over the threshold

and down the stairs

delivered in bottles

                      it was the milk

exploded

            they sent me to get it

cold

          and slippery

over my Dr. Dentons

onto the hard porch

                          tiny slivers

of glass

            and milk

like foam sloshing out of

my father's beer

                    all over

the table

            I wanted to lick it

like my cat

          maybe I'd bleed to death
and they'd be sorry

              but then
I smothered my cat
at least I took it to bed
and hid with it
            under the blanket

and that's what they told me

hated cats
        after

because I couldn't
           hate
              them

Black ink black paint

                    softening whiteness

as the body discovers itself
its folds and creases

              composed by the field

around it

       or is it the body

that composes the field

             its long hair

                  falling

and the garments trailing behind

transformed

          as if the naked back of a man

has altered the space he moves through

as if his presence in a dark wood
is the thickening absence
she needs to recover

           in her own dark

all morning Ruth and her paintings

we are trying to name

             her new show

unable to name what's back of
the deepening eddy
in the eyes

        or what any two hands
might be wanting to say

                    space and figure

it would have to make room
for what we find
             whiter
and more strange

                    for Ruth Nevo

The Floor Keeps Turning

                              thirty years
later

        I want to remember
how I stood
            with my children

and watched the great pendulum
knock down
                the little bronze pegs

or stood at the clock tower
in Prague when the tiny doors
                              opened

what do we mean
                  when we say time
stands still
            what does it wait for

the guests check out
                      fruit ripens
with no one to pick it

                    the sorrow
of melons rotting in rows

the way I wait for a phone call
that doesn't come

or my friend measures
three cups of water
for the packaged soup

                 and sits down
across from the place
               where he
used to be

she looks at her watch

AWAY

When I see such things, I'm no longer sure
that what's important
is more important than what's not.

WISŁAWA SZYMBORSKA

"Forgetting" he said coming back
to the table for his key

                "is a way of life"

a small neat man in a belt
and suspenders
           "my pills"
his wry little smile

            coming back
to share his forgetting with us

and none of us German

                sour cream
muffins after a night's sleep
and bitter coffee

           waiting to board
the next plane

        so then
we remembered
           where we were

and what we had wanted
             to forget

August 6
Frankfurt airport hotel

The sign on the new bridge

over the wreckage
reads
　　　high winds and wet soil
　　resulted in windthrow

　　　　　　　　uprooted
cedars like overreaching
　　　　　　　　　　towers
their Babel hubris

　　　　　　fir trunks
like ancient columns
　　　　　　　　thrown down
in the Cardo

　　　　　　the constant and awful
thinning out of lives

　　　　　　death
lets the light in

seedlings ferns small brush already
waist-high in the ruins

　　　　　　　　as if some
calculated wrath has ravished the woods
to let them grow

　　　　　　windthrow
rage and the soggy rubble

pale shoots already
                    nuzzle the sun

the rain forest shines

in its new
            immanence

                          beginning
(one place at least)
                    to heal

Cathedral Grove, Vancouver Island

Places I'm not allowed
whispers
        family secrets

                still
sharpen their pencils in me
to a fine point

           powdery graphite
thin spirals of wood

under the silk scarves
             Anthony Adverse
in my mother's drawer

             and Buddy
next to my old house
             unbuttoned
behind his garage door

tells me to watch
           his pee trickle
down the driveway

           killed
in the war

        the great elm
on the other side of the hedge
dividing our backyards
             gone too

and the tree house
where I watched the boys
            shimmy
up the trunk

        springy branches
hiding the trapdoor

        NO GIRLS

if only
    I peed like them

Seattle

They are all we are all

                        I am

well not exactly
               old

but not able to say what
happened
               yesterday morning

or as Cap put it over his crab cakes
at Madeline's
               seventy-seventh
birthday party

we never lose anything
but we spend a lot of time
               looking for it

Stan still remembered
               Jamison's
drugstore on the corner
                  chocolate
milk-shakes
             for only a nickel

I could taste the thick sweetness
feel the high stool
               hard
under my butt at the counter

you have to be old
                    to start
talking like that

                    so we watched
the sky fade

          till the red
was as pale as the thin slice of
pickled ginger on my plate

those of us not
seated with our backs to it

                         sunset
over Puget Sound
                    as it always was

September 3
Seattle

The city levitates
                              across the bay
where I left it

                    and over the bridge
the fog
          in its wispy departure
whiffles my loose ends

if I were looking for a sign
that's where I'd find it
                              high up
on the headland
                    over the golden gate
where you and I first

                    not where
I pass you the jam now

at somebody else's table
on somebody else's chairs

                         not with
Peet's coffee and toasted muffins

we are playing house
in the three bears' kitchen

turning our backs on whatever
snaps
          at our heels

but just when I think
we are clear
        and unrumpled

I'm back
      in the unmade bed

Berkeley

Thirty years since I wanted
my dreams back

why
didn't you ask me sooner
only last week
I cleaned out
my files

that's what he said

I could have killed him
but I'd already learned he wasn't
my father

now I'm under the water
riding to San Francisco
without
any dreams

and nothing to read
but a warning

IN CASE OF EMERGENCY
LOOK

LISTEN

RESPOND

CROSS OVER TO ADJACENT TRACK
AND WAIT FOR RESCUE TRAIN

I've already

        been rescued

                so why

am I looking in this tunnel

for my dreams

               Berkeley

They've rolled the parchment
again
      to its beginning

             I want
to feel a rolling
          under my feet
as if I am walking
        in sand

each point of arrival
          a stepping-stone

to the next oasis

        what if
there were a shorter way
through the wilderness
           would we
have arrived sooner
        and to
what

    Hittites
        Canaanites
    Shiites
        Pre-Raphaelites
    anchorites
        plebiscites

would they have

              .   opened

their arms to us and said

                              sister/brother

have some water

                (and some oil)

make yourselves

            at home

I strip myself

            of the past year

enter the hum

            of prayer

warm

            as an old sweater

pulled over my head

                              Rosh Hashanah
                                    Berkeley

The evil has been committed
the significant question is
                              who
will redeem it

                    the swell
of atonement
                    one day
                              a year

but who can forgive us

                              up there
on the pulpit

as if I were watching
two men in white knickers
                              somersault
on a high wire
                    lifting white shawls
like sails on the mindless water

to catch
          a lost breeze

                    light
exhales over the crowd
                              we are
laughing and cheering
                              (imploring
and praying)

               they bounce
on the wire
               out of touch
with the earth

we will have to fall back on

                    Yom Kippur
                    Berkeley

Unstoppable fury when you
switch on the radio

                              even
between the lines

commuter traffic
                    once more

watching the fog run
its fingers
              over the hills
on the other side of the bay

over the boxed glass
ubiquitous steel

the blue-gray shimmer
calms me
              blueberries in cream

and options
              still
                    open

                              Berkeley

JERUSALEM AGAIN

just enough to keep going

And then you were peeling
the first orange
                    still green
in October

                    the way you can
always
unbreakable ribbon
                        in your hands

juice oozing across our fingers
and our chins

                    wobbly
with jet lag
                    and longing

threshold:
what it can mean for two lovers
to wear down
                    a little
their own older threshold

                                dear drift
through the rooms dear shapes
unaltered

                    like sticks of incense
glowing

after all those
before them
the ones who will

but who will
come after
what trace of

our luggage unopened
at the door

October 16

Waking in bed in the shrill
dark
        sounds in my head
without language

                trying to
sort out the pieces

                matched
fragments
            held up
to a one-way mirror

October's quiver

                on our side
of the world
            she wrote
                    the trees
are astoundingly beautiful
so many shades of gold

                I've seen
those sun-dazzled aspens

                not like
the Calf the Dome the gilded
icons
        celestial ambitions
that have to go wrong

sacrificed bodies
                    under their flags

not under a blanket
as I am
            before dawn now

shivering

No rain yet

good news doesn't come

through the window

but the jacaranda

is more ferny than ever

filling

with so many birds

I don't know the names of

emergency cabinet meeting

a little too noisy

in the branches

a little too

philosophical

as in my beginning (twitter)

is my end

the birds are not

killing and dying

slightly unruly

they dive for my bread

their tiny heads dart

forward

and back

like Indian dancers

without any necks

a white-rumped jay
it's always a jay
           cries

countthedead
           countthedead

Because you have everything
                              (almost)
you need

            don't make a virtue
of detachment

                  talking to
myself again
                  because I don't
sing in the shower

                        because I nod
in a room filled with people
whose language I don't
understand

            ...*stretched between*
contemplation of a motionless point
and the command to be active
in history

                  the one I am talking to
is depressed
                  seriously
                              (maybe)

she can't get up in the morning
can't
      walk to the corner
to mail a letter

                    she's worthless
she tells me
no matter what anyone says

when we talk
                she works very hard
to keep her voice
                steady

we pull both ends of a long string
taut

        to measure a fence

Daily ritual

its own vocabulary

settling accounts

targets

strategic approach

assessing

the situation the goddamn
situation

everyone arguing at once

litter of legs

little torn legs
of the latest

Taha Muhammed Ali begins
his poem

what makes me love
being alive

he sells olivewood camels
to tourists in Nazareth

his book
walks barefoot

on *coins with holes*
at their center

bullet casings

old ladies' copper rings
thrown away by their grandsons

it is called *Never Mind*

                        I'm not sure
what (if)
        I love today
ask me next week

the world Ali says
                and *dreams*

On the wall next to my window

Masaccio's Adam and Eve

                              expelled

and unrestored

as I found them in Florence
vine leaves
                hiding their sex

driven
            over that threshold
into this world

                        Eve's anguish

open mouth
                from which the wail

first pain and first panic
first birthing cry

                        wherever

paradise is lost

a few cactus hedges
broken stones

                    our home was here

who
        will make art of this

Little love poem

        little undelivered

words

    for you
bringing milk tea to my desk
at ten in the morning
        predictable
as Japanese trains

       such good tea
fragrant and steamy

       breath of
a placable world in a cup

last night I was afraid
        to sleep
to lose my small claim
on things we depend on

        waited
for what would catch us
out of the dark
     unguarded

now
    tucked into your everyday
caring

I collect these words
like coins
in the bowls of beggars

they add up to
just enough to
keep going

Last fling of sundown
over the hills
                        raw flesh of salmon
dissolving

                my father
reeling them in
                        salt spray
and gulls

                the cypress
across the street
                        suddenly
black

            pump and pulse

the heart
                is not able to speak
without any words

                        (all of us talking
about how we feel)

                        let it say loss
say blame
                say today is
thanksgiving somewhere else

                                            no

let it speak plainly
in its own breath

              salt spray
and gulls
        the bright plume
after our small boat

            small
bamboo flute
         his quiet poems

at one with the water

it is always that simple

          for Sam Hamill
          Thanksgiving

What wants to continue
must not end
   says the *Wen Fu*

what wants to end
     must not
continue

   words from a box
each day
   that become our language

ESCALATION

    as if we were riding
on a staircase
   that only goes up

the real ones
   so small below us
we hardly see them

     pretty soon
we won't even hear their cries

there are times
   when the spirit freezes

I used to know how many years
light travels to reach us

I used to remember
                    more than I forgot

the kinds of grief
                    love teaches

nothing like this

sometimes a door slowly opens
sometimes the door remains bolted

Rachel's children are playing
war games
                empty plastic bottles
hurling them
                hard

they choose sides
                        good guys
bad
        what's the difference
if everyone fights

                        oh it's fun
to play war on the weekend
when nobody dies

                        the coffee drips
and I set out four cups

we are going to read poems
to one another
                re-vision
little intervals
                of flight

                        like seed
scattered at the end of winter

poems
        with their earnest overreaching

sorting the syllables

                in our mouths

even

      the soundless spaces

we crack them

          between our teeth

like they do

        at the movies

and spit the shells

           on the floor

for Rachel, Lisa, and Linda

I remember when Jesus wept
in Bethlehem

                    I saw it myself
said Father Anastasios
                              officially
declaring a new miracle

                              right there

candles and incense
                    the smoky painting
above the grotto of the nativity

he saw a tear
                    run down
from the right eye

they used to launch
                    white doves
from their cages
                    over Manger Square

no doves now
no miracles

                    at midnight
the plaster infant
                    under the altar
waits on his satin pillow
chalk-faced and smiling

fat legs

    frozen

        in the air

    Christmas Eve

The weatherman tells us
snow's on the way
                    to Mount Hermon
blown over from Europe

we have to get ready

                    I want
the wind to tear
                    the black thoughts
out of my head

                    and bury them
under the drifts
with all the lost causes

I want the whole sky
                    to lie down
on snow
            so that the only sound
is the hush
            of melting

I'm at the top of the lift
where everything's shining

the chairs
            rock by
without politicians

                        small hopes
bend their stiff knees again
as they start
                down the run

too frozen
                to know where
they're going

On clear nights I watch holes
open in the sky
                      light
trickles through

                        tiny strings
space shards
                 vibrating hair
of the cosmos

                   weightless specks
of discredited prayers

nothing forgives us in Jerusalem

we speak of
                 opening the mind
as if a door were closed
and we could unlock it

do you know what I'm saying

God almost touches Adam
but their fingers

                   stone walls
ditches barbed-wire fences

unbridgeable

                    what is it
we long for
                    what lifting
of the heart to change us

unsteady steps

how we tried it the first time
fell
        and got up
                        hammered
the air with our small fists

and stumbled again
our arms spread wide

over the
                        threshold

TWO

February

The park hangs on to what keeps growing
under the ice. Out of the whiteness
plum trees offer their affirmations.
The sky is clear and tremulously blue
around the leftover moon.
Early walkers let their dogs loose.

Crossing the hidden grass
we step out of our footprints in the frost.
What is it that glistens
like salt spray on your face,
that gathers like honey in a hive,

that makes our slow edging
to the end feel like
becoming?

The Emperor of China

I didn't know I was going to sleep until I woke up...
PAUL BOWLES

1

Remember the boy who played with a rope
in Kieslowski's film? He wrapped it around his hand
in the back of the taxi before he strangled the driver. Because.
Filmed through a filter, gray-green pallor of streets in a city,
moldy faces. Unnatural light the color of evil. It follows us now
when the sky is so steadily even in winter blue. Follows us
climbing the sanctified hill in Ein Kerem, the two mothers touching
each other's bellies, the unborn skimming across the valley
in their bees' wings, and a choir of children in the courtyard
of the Church of the Visitation singing Mozart.

2

Thin little squares of metal sewn in the hems of drapes
to make them hang straight. They are weighing me down.
Like the pigment and gravel in a Kiefer painting crushed
by the weight of its own excess. I don't want romance
in dungheaps, or Nuremberg with a blowtorch and traces
of blood. I don't want silence under the master's arches.
I want them to hear what I say. Disorder, chaos, the fibrillation
of my heart. I don't want us to fight the old wars.

3

"I was the eldest son of the Emperor of China. Our father
put me in a basket, summoned his mandarins in their funny caps
to rock me to sleep and fill me with nightmares about the war,
so when he died and I would be Emperor I'd be so scared

of war I'd never start one." When Uri was nine or ten in the camps
and his younger brother was frightened, he would tell him
the story again and again, how it all was a dream while he slept
in a basket and how nothing they went through was real.

4

"Enjoy your life," said our friend on her eightieth birthday,
"whether you like it or not." As we drive to the Peace
and Other Dreams Writers' Conference in Beersheba,
a blue glass *hamsa* dangles from the rearview mirror
against the evil eye. There are fields of sunflowers
on both sides of the road. Their quivering faces follow us
down the highway, rimmed with light. They will be harvested
for oil and seeds the birds haven't stolen. I'm glad for the yellow,
that it's not at the center, that it sways and shines all the way
to the edge as long as the eye remembers.

5

The shape of a sound, your voice and the vowels as I saw them
in the first years, lips slightly open over mine and your warm
tongue bringing me here. The place of beginnings. We never
thought about the End. Where we are is only where we have been.
Diamond edge of the mind, our selves coming out of the rock
like spiked thistles. Something older than bodies that live
for a moment under the blankets, their moist skin touching.
Diamond and coal the same pure element of carbon. How you
talked about Lawrence when we first met. I want you to feel my
heart at the back of your throat. We can't go on with the quarrels
near the rubble of the next war. If we could only remember
how we started, perhaps the words would remember us
the way we found the road home in a blackout.

6

Oh love, for the young wolf caught in a foot trap in Sinai
who pulled the trap out of the ground and dragged herself
with the trap attached over our border, now healed and set free
in the desert; for the red heifers they'll never breed pure enough;
for the tiny knuckles of freesia and hyacinth breaking out of
the cold earth before it is spring; for us in our cheerfulness
and fury, for days when we're still who we were from the beginning
unrecognized; for the Emperor of China, for dreaming and waking
though we're all dying, whether you like it or not, enjoy.

7

We're bent in the garden planting spring bulbs, pulling up
weeds, and I'm wondering how much longer we'll crouch here
on our knees in the damp soil sorting things out. Guardians
of shrubs and flowers. The first wild cyclamen sipping the sun.
We watch over each other as we watch over our garden,
woolly branches of cacti, fiery pokers of aloes in winter.
Especially during a long drought, after a snowfall, or following
the arcs of missiles on our screen. Flurries of extra caring.
Some mornings we hang on to each other as if we're afraid to let go.

8

What lasts is what we are up against. We are dividing
the city after the walls came down. Raising new barriers.
I explain why I did what I did you explain why you said
what you said and that makes it worse it gets obsessive
like our neighbor across the street who sweeps the stone path
to his front door every day and now that it's snowing
sweeps it every few hours. He's out there still in the numbing cold
wearing shorts black socks and sandals, making neat little mounds

of dirty snow. First he sweeps every pine needle out to the curb
and cleans up the sidewalk. Then he turns on the hose
and washes it down. We watch from our windows
as the soft flakes fall and he wipes them off with a rag,
wrings out the rag and wipes them again.

Ungaretti's Umbrella

Claude says, "This is
Ungaretti's umbrella," when he comes
to return a book. Comes
between rains, to keep
the umbrella dry.

Claude remembers thunder and hail
when Ungaretti read in Jerusalem,
but the words were quiet:
Isonzo... Serchio...
names of his rivers.

Everyone forgets umbrellas,
but this one is Ungaretti's.
The crook of the silver-rimmed handle
fits two hands. Claude says,
"Ungaretti was a small man."

What did he want
with such a huge black umbrella?
Outside the rain is falling again,
soft now as the threads of silkworms,
light filaments of hope.

The pines, the cypress,
the pepper trees across the road
rise up to meet it. The way
we'd rinse our minds if we could
from the unthinkable.

I make some tea. The umbrella
stands furled in the corner
like Captain Hook's black sleeve.
We still need a shelter
over our heads.

The Small Nouns

in memoriam, George Oppen

I wish I could tell you
that a whiteness made us
stop on the path
five smooth petals
close to the earth
they had hardly let go of
star-faced and slippery
small blaze at the center
noun of one
flower

When I went back
right after your death
I couldn't find it
the air was colder
flocks of swallows flew past
on their way to Africa
two ladybugs motionless
on a yellow leaf

I couldn't find it
no one had seen
a flower like that
in September
whatever it
was

Translation

1. *Outlet*

And what is the next move
(we're not playing checkers)
where do we go from here to
this evening
                    let's try it
one hour at a time
the sky full of suds
soapy water and sirens
or too much detergent
clogging the *outlet*

Meir says that *exit* is more
neutral
            as if outlets
for sewage into the Ganges
were more hopeful than
exits
        all the believers
filling their jugs and bottles
the way we keep filling our minds
with cures and promises
so at least we can
                    live   die
(how's that for neutral?)
looking for the right
                    word

2. *Wind*

Like the blast
that knocked down
the potted tree on our porch

or *spirit*
        old *ghost*
up there on the parapet
not wearing armor
but wrapped in the fury of
Cobras
        dead fathers
hissing their rage

what do we know
about revenge
            the night watch
cringes
      I feel my way
into the dark
the *wind* fled out of
(*spirit*   *ghost*)

and set the pot straight
bring you this small branch
broken:
        one lemon
almost ripe

3. *Figure out*

You have to be able to
hear the unknowable speak
if it isn't burning
something like that

in those days they listened
to whirlwinds or a burning bush
the trick was to *figure out*
who was The Voice

you don't *invent* someone
who already is

4. *Likely*

We never hear them
screams of the dead
shot down from planes
or helicopters
              blown up
in another city
knifed on a trail in the park

what do we think they sound like
how would they enter the clean
channels of our ears
              why do they
stay unheard in the mind
that asks such questions

do we want to *suppose* them

                            invent

what we can't imagine as resonance

or wails

          or even diminishing whimpers

how inviolate they are

in the words that seek them

even a shiver of *what must have been*

how noiseless the noise of the *likely*

    5. *Put aside*

Bitterness

          the swamp of it

sucking me deeper

viscous and dark as history

or bile

       dead leaves on a dead lawn

muddied with rain

remove it or *put* it *aside*

how can you come this far

after the ripening

and stay immobilized

as if a step forward

will be over the brink

                                        postpone it

surrender

                        in pleasure and dismay

benevolent whispers

angels' wings

        6. *Nibbling*

What would you do with an avocado

in your bed

                        swelling under the sheet

where it becomes all belly and hips

and you can only flatten

yourself on the softness

until you squash it

the small head on the pillow

bites to survive

                        no

gentler because it doesn't want

to give up the danger

                                the pleasure

of so much weight it can't bear

nibbling

                little nips and dares

and continental breakfasts

butter melting on a warm roll

7. Human vessel

Around the cape of no-hope
the *human* what-shall-we-call-it
sails

      not *ship* not *canoe*
not a beautiful pea green *boat*

but *vessel*
          the cargo in it small
as the wick of a candle on a leaf
lighting our way to the ghat

to be carried like that
on the treacherous water
flickering
         and poignant
as the documentation of nonevents

the Owl and the Pussy-cat
overwhelmed by their frailty

holding each other
when the wave breaks

The Lawns of Delhi

On the lawns of the Mogul Gardens,
on the lawns of the International Centre,

on the freshly mowed grass of all
the roundabouts in Delhi,

women squat in their saris
pulling up weeds.

They loosen the roots with their bony
fingers, pluck them out whole.

The women creeping on the cropped green
are small and bent. They squat

in the heat in their bright saris.
Their hands are dry twigs.

There is no shade but the shadow
of their bodies. How quiet they are.

Still crouching in back of my eyes
as they crouched over themselves.

Asparagus

When I saw the asparagus stand up in one bunch
as if they were waiting for the next train
stand up and then fall steaming on my plate
and when I saw how tender they were and young
as if they'd just been picked from the garden
and barely ripe with little scrubbed tufts at the end
like watercolor brushes I wanted to take the stalks
in my hand and bite off each tiny green tip
but what about Alice and then I remembered
picking my first asparagus in my friend's garden
crowded with overripe vegetables and blossoms
of cosmos blowsy and bruised on the ground
like large scoops of orange and strawberry sherbet
melted together and these were the only green
clusters. I snapped off a stalk sweet and crisp
in my mouth it tasted like nothing I'd forget.

Our friend is conducting some medical research
with a grant from Japan. He gets free trips
for testing the smell of the urine of people
who eat asparagus. He has a large sample group
and wants to find out why some urine stinks after
and some doesn't. When he told us about it
at the dinner table while eight of us were munching
on asparagus not exactly munching because
they were overcooked which they usually are
except in expensive restaurants somebody quickly
changed the subject so he didn't collect any data.

Sometimes I think I'm losing my grip on whatever's
important. Turning my windshield wipers on and off
and on again when the rain and the sun get mixed up
and the sky can't decide to be gray or blue
doesn't help much to settle my own confusion
or clear any thickets in my soul
or make any difference when Sarah tells me
that she's learned in Philosophy 101
we don't know whether we have free will
because we don't know whether we don't have it.
I was never a judge of what matters
that's only for God and rare children and certainly
not for the ones with the answers. The rest of us
have to watch where we're going or simply make do.

THREE

Listening

You told it softly, not looking at my face,
how you'd been lost a long time
from where you had started,

the earth packed hard with light,
your child curled in the shadow
where he lay, so that the hum

of insects was the hum of the desert
tracked by buzzards, everything waiting
out there to fatten on death.

More than flower power, more than
Joplin or Hendrix, more than anything else
that happened while I was trying not

to get older, I remember his end
in your arms in Mexico after
you left the commune, fifteen hours

of talking until the sun came up,
the sun he perfected himself to live by,
cleansing the brain the flesh the spaces

in every cell, so purified from starving
only the sun could enter. A mind
of cinders. Babbling like the sibyls.

And I remember my own self, feeding
on somebody else's grief, wanting
to live it again as my own life,

as if that would change me or help me
listen with my body to the real world —
the simple hunger of the child.

Jump

Sundays. Sun-narrowed eyes. My father
in the leaky rowboat unties the frayed rope
from its peg, raises his arm from the oar
he steadies and holds out his hand. My job
is to bail out the water when the dinghy leaks.
One foot in the boat, one foot on the dock:
the lake quickly widens under my crotch.
When he cries *Jump*, I jump, and fall in.

I've narrowed the distance, reach for him
now in his vagueness, honey on his tongue
and the songs of Zion. What did he know
about this hot wind breathing down my neck
like the future — stripping the sand from the desert?
A bright face blown off. Out there in the light
as far as my eyes can see there is only
what's happened.

            If I could scoop out the water
with my small can. I am filled with intentions.
My father says *Jump*. When I get to one side
what I want most is on the other.

Seattle–Jerusalem

A Sheet of Foil

First day of spring on the Hill of Anemones, masses of scarlet,
pink and deep purple, the blood of Adonis seeping
into the earth. Hatched by the sun, they widen their mouths
and tilt backwards to take the light in, fields brimming
all the way to the village on the next hill. Wildflowers,
stones, everything warming in its ancient bed. Even
the chill between us. My mother smiles, I nod my head
to acknowledge the endlessness of the dead. To let her know

I remember we sat on the floor together while she cut the wings
and glued them on cardboard and fastened them to my shoulders.
Shimmering gold foil. I was the angel she pasted in scrapbooks.
She goes on turning the pages without me. Sometimes
I find myself in a room I've entered forgetting what for.
Or I could say each place I return to is changed. That's why
the slope in front of the house I grew up in was steeper before.
When I spread my arms at the top of our stairs, I flew.

Grow old along with me! The best is yet to be. My mother read me
her favorite poem from the leather-bound gilt-edged book
her first love gave her. The leather was green as pine boughs,
soft as my pillow when I pressed my finger in it. I could feel
his breath on her skin. So this was poetry. I heard the music
as if from the throats of flowers, angels sirens mermaids Mother
singing next to my father while he drove, *All of me, why not take*
all of me? Bel canto with a little kvetch. Her eyes were cinnamon,

blurry with tears the day I caught her over my diary, and bellowed
my hate. Fifteen and furious, her only child crazy with breasts,
she like a creeper, fastening. Nechama. Her name meant comfort.
Not in the doctors' waiting rooms. Not in the cigar smoke
sanctum of his poker nights. Not in her anguish of pleasing.
But there in the picture between her sisters holding me on the
canvas swing. Tender and blameless. We rock in the backyard
under the willow. Comfort ye, comfort ye, says the prophet.

When I walk in the dry riverbed, the crunch of my sandals
is the sound of childhood, running along the beach in summer.
Surf at the edge, like the swish of a thin sheet of foil
as it wrinkles and folds on itself. She keeps smoothing it out.
This isn't my childhood, and I move here cautious under the steep
cliffs, the layers of sediment. The way I walk between
closely packed graves, not to profane what's under them.
Not to disturb her fingers at my back, steadying the wings.

Jerusalem–Seattle

The Haunting

If all she remembered at the end
was hate I spit at her
when I was fifteen, wild
and unforgiving, only to get it back
in fistfuls from my own child,

if all my burnt offerings,
grass fires across the years
left failure in their wake
where nothing could grow,

now when my daughter hums
a strange solace and her fingers
pluck at the strings until the music
sings from the gleaming belly of the oud
as clear as insight or the first rain,

what, from her ghostly distance,
does she hear, what
does she see when I look
at my daughter with her eyes?

Shell-Flowers

Like the turkeys you raise each year
I visit you fattened and older, fighting
to save my neck. I can't speak
your ineffable language. As if your soul
in its radiance has nothing to prove.
Like God. Though you have renamed him.
Was he in you already and only to be found?
Or did he come last year and take you
when you circled the Ka'ba seven times?

We manage somehow. Black scarf
fastened under your chin to hide
your hair. My grandmother in her wig.
Because only women can be shamed.
Musty petals as they brushed my cheek,
her lips trembled with psalms. She stirred
the soup with her daughters during the Seder
while the men shook the plagues from their fingers
and drank the wine.

                    When you were small
I sat on your bed and read to you
about the exquisite web a pig watched over.
The glow of the lamp on your rapt face.
I gave you shell-flowers, snug little magic
pockets that sank to the bottom of the glass.
A burst of crimson up through the water
on a green thread wagging its tissue-paper leaves.
A leap of faith. I didn't know
how far it would carry you.

Islands

The sea is as calm as a good wife,
absorbed in itself.

Islands hidden all morning
in a blue haze.

Bare-breasted women are oiling
their shoulders.

I'm listening to the one-note blues
of cicadas lost in the pines,

after so many years still listening
to sirens, unaccountable screams.

What are we doing on the sand
with our eyes closed,

hiding out like the first time,
unsure of each other,

astonished lovers whispering,
What happens next?

Little Late Marriage Poem

I was never young with you
except in the ways you saw me

or I thought of myself
making love so close to the edge

of the bed we fell on the floor
and laughed till we cried.

If we aren't always
moving toward each other

at least we seem to be going
in the same direction.

Chartreuse

Far away in the French Alps near Grenoble the Carthusian monks
are making Chartreuse. I don't know if Chartreuse would taste
any different if one of the hundred and thirty herbs and flowers
were missing or the monks spoke to one another more than one
hour a week. Would it matter if a monk spoke for two hours? Or
a flower became extinct? Would the liqueur be a greener yellow,
a yellower green? Sometimes when you tell the story of how you
arrived in Palestine in '48 as the British pulled out of Lydda and
you had to be rescued, you forget the part about the soldier sit-
ting on your knee all the way to Tel-Aviv, your one hand itching
at her soft waist, the other one balancing a grenade. Each year
the variables increase, we lose a little bit more of our earthlight.
I can't help wanting your story again without explosives, a hun-
dred and thirty herbs and flowers, your arms around me when
the airport falls, if it isn't the life we expected, something close.

FOUR

In the Beginning

When he wakes, he turns
on his side. Something
is missing.

Already she's out in the garden
smelling the lilacs, naming
the pterodactyls.

Already she's claiming
the strange face rippled
in the pond,

a terrible eagerness, trying
to scoop the pale shape
into her hands.

It's only water.
She wants it to tell her
who she is, or

what he lost.

The Death of Rachel

All day she stirs the soup
while the tourists park their cars
on the side of the road to visit
her tomb. Soldiers stand guard.
Barren women sway in their scarves
and pray for a child.
She stirs bitter lumps
from the dry riverbed
where the sheep feed on anything
that grows. She keeps her eyes
on the pot so it won't boil over.

When she stole her father's idols
and he chased after them,
she sat on the gods. She told him
the slit moon under her skirt
spilled blood and she couldn't rise.

She's run out of lies.
She has been ready for a long time
listening to the calm of the desert
between her pains.
She strains till the last one in her
forces his dark head out.
She stirs the dust into dust.

Yael

Then Yael... took a hammer in her hand,
and went softly unto him...
JUDGES 4:21

She must be an angel, waiting outside
with the tent flap open.
He has to stop there, half dead,
running so far from the battle,
the chariots lost.
He enters the shelter of her wings.

She gives him milk
and covers his trembling with her robe.
Reckless, she lies down beside his fever.
His breath burns in her cool mouth.
His hands stammer
across her body.

If she'd been painted in the act
like Judith by one of the great ones,
we might have known her
sprawled in disheveled ardor,
or driving the tent-pin
through his skull.

All summer she's followed the sheep,
dry grass along the dry rivers,
while the men sharpen their sticks
with the men. The sweet
brutality she's servant to. Sisera sleeps.
She knows what she has to do.

Job's Wife

She has to pity him after what happened,
rocking alone like that in the rubble,
covered with boils. She's watched him scrape
his sores with anything broken, half naked
and bleeding, scraping his soul.

And if she staggers out of the dark
to hound him when he is busy
with his own grief, surely he'll speak
for her too, three daughters, seven sons,
aren't they in this together?

She's wearing the slip she had on
when the house was blitzed and everything
with it: children, donkeys, we know
how many. And how, with nothing to lose,
she begs him to damn God and die.

He's all that's left, beyond what they
used to be for each other, abuse
or solace. He scratches his scabs
and tells her she's foolish. She stares
at the unrelenting sky.

Unfinished Poem

We live on a holy mountain
where the crows and the Crowne Plaza
rise higher than our expectations

and the golden dome is only
a restored reflection
of the absolute.

All night the bodies of prophets
break out of the clouds
calling, "Doom, doom."

Like the carp we bring home
from the market, our lives
are wrapped up in newsprint.

My friend says she'd like to
cut off her head and let all
the Jewish history run out.

We lift weights together
twice a week to increase
our bone density.

for Lois

Ladders

When the angels were too old
to climb up and down their ladders,
they would suck in their breath,

unroll their wings, and blow
themselves to the next rung.
Until even that didn't go.

Like turning a key on a toy bird
after the battery is dead.
They got rid of the ladders.

With God it's worse. He forgets
all the ladders are gone.
He forgets that he forgets.

He does what he does best:
calling us for the sacrifice,
his ineluctable test,

as if times hadn't changed, as if
we could count on a ram in the thicket
or stop the knife.

Hubris

The loom is computerized.
He has already woven
the robe for the priest,
and the pants, like the robe,
one seamless garment.

She's spinning the thread
and weaving the cloth
for the thirty-two-meter girdle.

They've finished the silver cup
for the sacrifice, large enough
for the blood of a large cow.

After they breed the red heifers
(only their ashes are pure enough),
after they score the still unheard music,
after the eleven spices are gathered
in separate jars
and the golden crown
and the solid gold menorah
and the lottery box
for the two goats,

and after they raise to perfection
the purest boy for the High Priest,
teach him The Immutable Law,

where will they hide him
when the Romans come?

FIVE

After

in memory of J.E.D. (1948-1995)

We had been looking at an idol in a glass case,
size of a hand, admiring her tough little knobs
and the ball of her belly some barren woman
prayed to and rubbed. He said
she had been holding up her breasts
for eight thousand years.

Sun flickers through the pine trees,
my daughter beside me, we are crying
and holding each other, putting stones
on your daughter's grave.

After the flaming rib cage of the bus,
after each string of flesh has been found
and collected according to the Law,
after they show it and show it and show it
until we can smell the muck in our room
and the roasted skin, after the street
is washed clean with a blast of water,
and after the reading of the names,

there is absence, unreadable.

Immersion

for the drowned Jews of Hania, Crete

The sound is not human
but I try to repeat it from my puckered lips
       plip
more pear-shaped than that   more open
tiny assertion
          not exactly plip
soft slap
      slip of one drop
of water into a pool
rainwater sliding off the tip of a leaf

one drop and another
the circles quiver
           ring within ring
until there's a whirl in the center
through which she enters the mikvah
one step at a time

through which their bodies fall

———

Not like our edging
toward the space where everything happens
for the last time
         not like the ink
draining out of the newsprint

into our breakfast
                    we eat it
and eat it
                whatever we might have done
and didn't

            springwater
bubbles through the floor
unschooled by gravity

———

Beginnings we long for
                        amniotic fluid
that cushioned our first lives
rebirth without pain
a coming into the light again
as if for the first time first wonder first
love of a human face

———

In the sanctuary
a drawer left open
with an antique key
                to what

———

Only a dark shaft under the tiny hinged door
on the stone floor of the synagogue
cut deep into the earth
a narrow tunnel the width of an arm
how far does it go

        how many scrolls and pages
have been rolled and fitted into that darkness
how much everyday holiness

they buried the words like precious children

———

Bodies
     what's left of four rabbis
in the swept yard what's left of
their scattered bones
       gathered
and buried again beyond embellishment

the blessings the prayers the vows
float in the air around them
names cut into granite
       still readable
under the bent willows brushing
the stone
     sunny cheeks of nasturtiums
dazzle of bougainvillea

———

And a brass ladle
placed like a sundial on the wall
to mark the hours
its shadow lengthens and moves
in a clock's direction
                              reversing itself
like a swirl of water
like time rolling backwards
where there is no time

ladle she dipped in the living water
to purify her soul

———

The great guile of faith
shivers the pool

one more pinch of the heart
she stands at the top of the stairs
and waits for a sign

———

Night lowers its blackout shades
over the outer wall
                              spliced reels
turn on their axis until dawn
wind and rewind

ripped out of
their family pictures
their battered affection
sagging with bundles

a netful of freshly caught fish
dragged back to the harbor
they choke on their names
straining to hear the last syllables
of connection
                    to keep them
from bronze plaques
lizards will sleep on

pieces of bread
clutched by the children
their mothers' fingers

one sad-eyed boy in the foreground
falls off the edge

———

Now a ghost figure rises like a half-moon
drifting out of the dark
it has a face
                    then a brighter face
and behind it another
it has become a white scarf covering the head
of a woman who drifts to the surface
where her bridegroom waits

he is running beside her
I look at his cautious mouth
I look in the dark shafts of her eyes
where the scrolls are buried
steep absence of light

———

Circles tighten around them
like exile like chimneys like
the hold of a ship
                    or time
in its helix repeating itself

they sink into history
with hardly a ripple

———

Black plume of smoke dissolving
where the ship was
                        mist rising
from the wreckage
their trapped cries

———

This is the way to the mikvah
this is the way
                    plip
this is

her foot in the cool water
how it trembles over her ankles thighs
the secret passage into her center
                              plip
her belly the white curve of her breasts
cleansed in the hallowed water
the beat of her heart the pulse in her throat
clarity
          in her held breath and the final
immersion of her head
she is weightless and buoyant
silkiness flows around her

———

Light from the wooden grille at the window
arranges its petals on the stone

Sanctum

1

On top of a hill near the Lebanese border,
Micha Ullman dug a grave, then cut through
the rocky outcrop and sculpted a throne.
As if he'd uncovered its archetypal shape
out of pure limestone.
                                    He raised the throne
and tilted it backwards, wedged between rocks
on both sides of the grave. A throne to lean back on
(if you dared) facing the overwhelming sky,
trusting the stone to bear your weight, suspended
over your own death.

                                    Once he dug holes
in Israeli and Arab villages, and filled each with earth
from the other. It was '73. Right after the war.
We lived on a cul-de-sac called *Neve Sha'anan*.
Place of Tranquillity. That too was conceptual art.

2

Houses across the road where I live now
are set back from the street, stone from ancient quarries
hewn and fitted together like giant bricks:
yellow rind and flesh of casaba
in the first slice of morning, color of milk tea
with a spoonful of honey at noon when the light is strong,
rose quartz at dusk.

To live in Jerusalem is to feel
the weight of stones. Stone walls around the City.
Solemn stones in the digs. Hard-hitting stones.
Names chiseled on stone lids over the dead.

Look on my works, ye Mighty, and despair!
That bleakness when I walk through ruins below
the Temple Mount/Haram al-Sharif,
below the sun and moon of the Dome and Al-Aqsa,
when I touch the colossal stones hurled down
by the Romans who smashed the Temple and sacked the city,
when I lay the palm of my hand on pitted history.

3

Sometimes, writing, I watch the words grow heavy
when I place them in rows on the page.
Deliver me from a city built on the site of a more ancient city,
whose materials are ruins, whose gardens cemeteries.
Whose people are desperate in their claims.

Sometimes I need to be nowhere. A place
without history.
                    A life of wandering
like the desert generation of Moses.
The wandering Jew. But that brings me
back into history.
                    Sealed rooms. Windows
crisscrossed with tape so the glass won't shatter.
A dark noose of memory around my neck.
Coffins covered with flags and flags
burning. I need to be nowhere.

4

The first time I climbed the road to the sculpture garden
to find Turrell's stone sanctum, *Space That Sees,*
I went alone. Entered the narrow passage, fingers
sliding across the cool stones. Arrived in a bare room
radiant with light.

                       Isn't that how they always begin,
the delicious stories? Through a secret passage, up
a beanstalk, down a hole.

                           Cut into the ceiling
was one square opening. When I looked up
the sky looked down entirely empty,
more blue than any blue dazzle outside.
All the unblemished blueness of a Mediterranean
summer in one clear window. No glass. No screen.
Nothing between.

                      I sat on the ledge tucked into
the stone surrounding me, stared till the light
became pulse and substance, and I could taste
its language in my mouth. There was no end to it.

During the Vietnam War James Turrell was jailed
and placed in solitary confinement. His cell so cramped
that he could neither lie down nor stand. Dark
as the bottom of a well. He could see nothing.
But strangely he discovered *there never is no light*
...even when light is gone you can still sense light.

5

I walk from my home in changing seasons, down
through the Valley of the Cross, up the path
through the olive trees to the gardens surrounding
that room. Often thin wisps of clouds leave
a smoke trail across the blue square over my head,
or clusters of vapor form and dissolve the way
thoughts quicken with words before I lose them.

I have seen two ravens cross in an instant and disappear
beyond the frame. I have seen the sky-space in silence.
And with a child who shouted to break the silence.
Once, lying down on the ledge, stretching my body
on the stone, I saw it as newly dyed cloth in India,
still wet and silky, spread out on the air to dry.

It has become the eye in the center of my head,
the eye of the vastness around it.
I have seen the movement of the unseen sun.
How shadows change on the interior wall.
As I have changed.
                        What is there out there
watching over me? Watching me watching it?

6

You and I on the stone ledge.

The immensity of space watching
through one small window the immensity of our failures.

Let's sit here together on the throne
as if suspended over our own deaths.
Let's lean back — easy — against the supporting stone,
and trust it to bear our weight

a little longer.

Notes

ONE: THRESHOLD

"You can feel the rising" (pages 13-14)

> Italicized words from Jane Hirshfield, *Nine Gates*, 1998.

"They've rolled the parchment" (pages 44-45)

> Italicized words from Seamus Heaney, Nobel Prize speech, 1995.

> *Rosh Hashanah:* The Jewish New Year, according to the Jewish calendar.

"The evil has been committed" (pages 46-47)

> Italicized words from George Seferis, *Days of 1945-1951: A Poet's Journal*, translated by Athan Anagnostopoulos, 1974.

> *Yom Kippur:* The Day of Atonement, the holiest day in the Jewish year.

"And then you were peeling" (pages 51-52)

> Italicized words from Rainer Maria Rilke, "The Ninth Elegy," *Duino Elegies*. My own translation.

"Because you have everything" (pages 57-58)

> Italicized words from Czeslaw Milosz, *Native Realm*, translated by Catherine S. Leach, 1968.

"Daily ritual" (pages 59-60) and "On the wall next to my window" (page 61)

> Italicized words from Taha Muhammed Ali, *Never Mind: Twenty Poems and a Story*, translated by Gabriel Levin, 2000.

"Last fling of sundown" (pages 64-65)

> Italicized words from Sam Hamill, "Heart of Bamboo" (*Gratitude*, 1998), as recorded in *Heart of Bamboo* CD, 1999, with Christopher Yohmei Blasdel playing the *shakuhachi* (bamboo flute).

"What wants to continue" (pages 66-67)

> Italicized words from Lu Chi's *Wen Fu, The Art of Writing*, translated by Sam Hamill, revised 1991.

"Translation" (pages 87–92)

> These seven poems came out of my translations from the Hebrew
> poetry of Meir Wieseltier (*The Flower of Anarchy: Selected Poems,*
> 2003). I selected seven Hebrew words I'd struggled with, and let the
> words, with their alternative possibilities in English and something
> of their context, create their own poems.

FIVE

"Immersion" (pages 122–128)

> In June 1944 a British submarine torpedoed and sank a German
> ship in the Sea of Crete, unaware that it was carrying the last of the
> Jewish community of Hania — two hundred and seventy-six men,
> women, and children — to Auschwitz. Jews had been living in Crete
> and worshiping in their synagogues for more than two thousand
> years. The Etz Hayyim (Tree of Life) Synagogue of Hania, their only
> remaining cultural center and place of worship, was desecrated,
> vandalized, and finally stripped and used for trash. It was reno-
> vated, together with its mikvah (ritual bath) and courtyards, under
> the direction of Nikos Stavroulakis and the support of the World
> Monument Fund, reopened in 1999, and rededicated in 2001 with a
> sculptural installation by David Behar Perahia. Many of the images
> of the poem were inspired by Perahia's installation.
>
> *Mikvah*: A sacred water immersion place where many religiously
> observant Jews immerse themselves regularly to become ritually
> and spiritually clean.

"Sanctum" (pages 129–133)

> The poem is based on my essay "Sky-Space and Stone," published
> in *Mānoa* 9:1, 1997.
>
> *"Look on my works..."* (page 130): "Ozymandias," Shelley.
>
> *"Deliver me from a city..."* (page 130): *Walden*, Chapter 14, Thoreau.

Acknowledgments

Our gratitude to the editors of the following publications, where some of these poems, often in earlier versions, first appeared:

American Poetry Review

Barnabe Mountain Review

Bridges

Field

Judaism

Kerem

Leviathan Quarterly

Natural Bridge

The Paris Review

Runes

Speakeasy

Stand

The Threepenny Review

TriQuarterly

Western Humanities Review

Southern Lights, the Anthology of PEN American Center/South, 1998

The Best American Poetry 2001, edited by Robert Hass and David Lehman, Scribner, New York, 2001

Inventions of Farewell: A Book of Elegies, edited by Sandra M. Gilbert, W.W. Norton & Company, New York, 2001

To Stanley Kunitz, with Love, edited by Stanley Moss, The Sheep Meadow Press, New York, 2002

A selection of poems from *Roots in the Air: New and Selected Poems* and from *Threshold* were reprinted together with French translations by Claude Vigée, in a bilingual edition: *Un Abri pour nos têtes,* Cheyne éditeur, Le Chambon-sur-Lignon, 2003

About the Author

Shirley Kaufman's earliest collection of poems, *The Floor Keeps Turning*, won the first-book award of the International Poetry Forum in Pittsburgh in 1969. Since then seven more volumes of her poems have appeared in English, including *Roots in the Air: New and Selected Poems*. She has also published books of translations of contemporary Hebrew poetry, by Abba Kovner and Amir Gilboa, and collaborated with Judith Herzberg on the translation of Herzberg's Dutch poems, *But What: Selected Poems*, which won a Columbia University Translation Prize. She recently co-edited, and translated with others, *The Defiant Muse: Hebrew Feminist Poems from Antiquity to the Present*. Her latest book of Hebrew translations is *The Flower of Anarchy: Selected Poems of Meir Wieseltier*.

Among her honors are fellowships from the National Endowment for the Arts and the Rockefeller Foundation, and the Shelley Memorial Award from the Poetry Society of America. A former resident of and frequent visitor to Seattle and San Francisco, she has lived in Jerusalem with her husband, H.M. (Bill) Daleski, since 1973.

The Chinese character for poetry is made up of two parts: "word" and "temple." It also serves as pressmark for Copper Canyon Press. Founded in 1972, Copper Canyon Press remains dedicated to publishing poetry exclusively, from Nobel laureates to new and emerging authors. The Press thrives with the generous patronage of readers, writers, booksellers, librarians, teachers, students, and funders — everyone who shares the conviction that poetry invigorates the language and sharpens our appreciation of the world.

PUBLISHERS' CIRCLE

The Allen Foundation for the Arts
Lannan Foundation
National Endowment for the Arts

EDITORS' CIRCLE

Thatcher Bailey
The Breneman Jaech Foundation
Cynthia Hartwig and Tom Booster
Target Stores
Emily Warn and Daj Oberg
Washington State Arts Commission

The publication of this book is also made possible with the generosity of
ALBERT AND JANET SCHULTZ PHILANTHROPIC FUND
THE BLOOMFIELD FAMILY FOUNDATION

For information and catalogs:

COPPER CANYON PRESS
Post Office Box 271
Port Townsend, Washington 98368
360/385-4925
www.coppercanyonpress.org

Threshold is set in Kepler, a Multiple
Master font designed by Robert Slimbach.
Multiple Master fonts can be varied —
in Kepler's case by weight, width, and set
size — to create unique instances of the
face. Here, the lightest weight, a medium
width, and exact set-size settings were
chosen for each size used in the text.
Then the fonts were generated and
appeared on the menu to be applied.
The title and section heads use a heavier
weight with the same width as the text.
Book design and composition by Valerie
Brewster, Scribe Typography. Printed on
archival-quality Glatfelter Author's Text
at McNaughton & Gunn, Inc.